Legacy Questions

867 Prompts to Start Your Memoir

ALSO BY CHRISTINA DREVE YOUNG

*My Feelings Journal: With Guided Exercises and a
Word Bank of 2000 Emotions*

Adventure Journaling: A Compass for Self-Discovery

*Write Your First Book in 30 Days: Get Ready,
Get Support, and Get Writing*

*Write Your Novel in November: Last-Minute Mind Tricks and
Shortcuts I've Learned from NaNoWriMo*

Rides to Remember: Your Motorcycle Log Book

Legacy Questions

867 Prompts to Start Your Memoir

CHRISTINA DREVE YOUNG

Copper Canopy Press
www.coppercanopypress.com

ISBN-13: 978-0-9967760-9-7

In all the world there's no one like you.

Use this book to share the story that only you can tell.

CONTENTS

FOREWORD

When I worked as a hearing aid specialist, most of my clients were over the age of 65. Because I saw them over a period of years, I was privileged to hear many stories.

These folks were retired, and sometimes they were lonely. I've always been a great listener, and I enjoyed spending time with each person. Despite a busy practice, I'd often book a fifteen-minute service into a thirty-minute slot so we'd have time to chat.

My clients told me stories their own kids hadn't heard. An Army pilot described weaving through mountaintops when he flew the hump in World War II. A widow explained her start in a 15,000 episode children's television show in Cincinnati. Another 83 year old even mentioned seeing UFOs in Denmark.

It became clear that some incredible memories might be lost forever without someone to listen. That prompted me to write down questions as quickly as I could. If you know someone with fantastic tales (or you have some of your own) this book is for you. I want to encourage you to share your experiences, and write your story for your legacy, and your grandchildren too.

INTRODUCTION

Some things seem too delicate to discuss. Force of habit can limit conversations with our parents, friends, and even our own adult children. Every family is different, but it's basic human survival to ignore emotional pain. You may worry that asking questions will dig up past hurts. The good news? Healing that can still happen no matter your age or stage in life.

There will come a time when you no longer have your friends and family members, and you'll think of things you wish you knew about them. You don't know those questions yet because that situation hasn't occurred. This book will let you ask some of those questions now.

Writing out memories of your own can also be enjoyable. You can linger in the happy times, and use "creative license" if you want to add a little color to the details. Let these questions guide you to the stories you most want to share. Even if you use just one prompt from this book, that's enough. There's no pressure to answer every question, or even to read the whole book. Use this however you wish.

If you have a loved one struggling with memory problems or who grows tired easily, start the conversation now. There are ways to stimulate memories, and you can try sharing some of your own first. It may seem frustrating for them to carry on a conversation, but they want to talk with you despite their difficulties. This is the moment you are waiting for...the opportunity for mom or dad to give voice to what's going on inside their head.

The questions in this book cover 12 different subjects and periods in life. You can skip entire sections, or go through every one of the 867 questions. This is just a place to start. You can skim the questions at home, and ask whatever comes to mind in your next visit. It is true that some people may not want to be interviewed on camera, but they may agree to have their voice recorded. With the size of smart phones now, it's possible to set up video without being intrusive. After all, you are not asking anyone to perform; you're simply having a conversation that you'll be able to listen to later.

Maybe it's easier to ask happy questions on camera and let conversations turn to other subjects once the camera is off. Perhaps you won't record any of the conversations, but use the questions to learn more about someone you've known for a long time. There is always more to know!

You've probably heard an older family member say they're bored or they feel useless. One of my friends told me since he turned 80, he's not even allowed to unload his own groceries. He understands that his adult children are trying to prevent injuries, but this has also made him feel helpless.

There is no greater gift you can offer friends and family members than the gift of your time. Being with them and asking questions shows you value them even if they're retired now. Your interest tells them they are still important to you and their experiences are valid. In addition to hearing some amazing stories, you'll likely hear things you've never heard before.

HOW TO INTERVIEW

Although you've been part of a family for years, there is still more to know. Some habits and relationship dynamics are so ingrained they often operate behind the scenes. You may think you know what someone will say to you, or believe certain topics that are forbidden. This is not always true.

As an adult, you've made choices in your life. Some were difficult or even impossible, and it's the same for your interviewee. These may be the most meaningful discussions you could have. Perhaps you can look at your own life and see choices that would have been better. Have you ever apologized to someone for your mistake? It's likely your interviewee has similar regrets, and sharing those regrets could lift an enormous burden. You may not be the injured party, but being able to verbalize and process those events out loud can be extremely helpful.

You can begin with factual questions like their birthdate and the city they were born. Ask their parent's names, grandparent's names, and any other great-grandparent's names they know.

Try to ask open-ended questions that lead to descriptions, not just yes and no questions. Also, allow them time to think. This is probably the hardest part of being an interviewer. When you ask about the faraway past, it takes time to re-forge mental connections and retrieve long dormant information.

Your family member may not notice the period of quiet that naturally occurs while they are formulating an answer. It's important to allow long periods of silence to occur. You are the only one who may feel awkward about the quiet, so maintain a relaxed and calm posture to support your family member as they think. Several minutes could pass in silence. Be respectful, and do not break into their thoughts to help them. Let them come up with the words they want to use and let them tell the story they want to tell.

Because we may be caring for a relative who has been through a stroke or memory problems, our habit may be to supply words or thoughts to jump-start them. If you see your family member becoming frustrated, it may be time for a break. You could also circle back to a fact-based question about a date or a location you'd like to know more about.

The other way to encourage discussion is a follow-up question. Here is a list of a few easy ways to ask more.

"Tell me more about that."

"Could you say more about (that topic)?"

"And then what happened?"

"What did you do next?"

"Do you remember anything else?"

"Is there anything else about that time (or place, or person) that you want to share?"

"How did you feel about it at the time?"

"How do you feel about it now looking back?"

"Why do you think that was so important at the time?"

"How is it to think about that again?"

"Why do you think you have remembered that for so long?"

"Can you give me some more examples of that?"

"Talk a little more about that"

"What was that like for you?"

"Describe that in your own words."

Your tone of voice is important when you ask these questions. Try to take the role of a neutral observer without judging their recollections and stories. If you know they are mis-remembering facts, or things didn't occur as they say, it is essential NOT to correct them right now. Act as a reporter who is getting an eyewitness account of events as they occurred. We know that witnesses notice some things, and miss other things entirely.

Staying neutral and supportive will encourage your friend or family member to share more freely. This may be your one and only opportunity to let them shine. Allow yourself to get to know them better and connect with them in a new way.

Approach these questions as a doorknob...they lead to new rooms and places you haven't been before.

You can follow-up on what you think may be inaccurate with another question. "I've heard that (whatever you believed was true), what do you think about it?"

As you sit with them, encourage them with eye contact and focused attention. Feel free to nod your head and smile. Try not to give a verbal "mm-hmm", say "yes", or make any kind of sound while they are talking. (In the playback of an audio or video interview, it is distracting.)

Keep a notepad with you. When you hear something that sparks other questions, jot those down and allow them to continue their story. When they seem to have exhausted the topic, ask your follow-up questions. This is where it can be hard to avoid your own bias. Instead of asking a leading question like "Were you angry when that happened?" ask how they felt, or if their feelings about something surprised them.

Another way to interview is ask about things you already know. Since you're looking to preserve memories, include day-to-day life. Describe the "old ways" of outhouses or homes without electricity. Where did food and clothing come from? Why do you need to travel now, and how do you get there? Something obvious to you could be fascinating to your future reader.

USE THESE QUESTIONS FOR YOURSELF

You can also ask yourself these questions. You don't have to share every detail, just what you want to tell. Pick the questions that make you react emotionally… there's probably a story behind that reaction. You can voice record your answers, or use your computer to type it out. Let one thought lead to the next, and do not edit as you write.

Let yourself observe these memories as if they were on a movie screen. Feel free to write whatever you wish, since you have complete control over what happens next to your content. (You may never show it to anyone, and that would be perfectly fine.) One approach to your story is to let go of any emotional "hold" the past may have over you and simply enjoy the best times all over again.

It's important to follow the memories without editing or deleting what you wrote. Let your thoughts flow through your fingertips and onto the page. There may be a reason to recount that story, so let yourself explore that time and place from the past.

If you find you are upset about some of the memories, it's useful to know the past really is over. Feeling emotions sometimes makes us judge ourselves. Are you still berating yourself for something long ago?

Here are two of my favorite books about reconciling the past:

Loving What Is: Four Questions That Can Change Your Life by Byron Katie

You Can Heal Your Life by Louise Hay

HOW TO PRESERVE MEMORIES

If you'd like to write out your answers, there are several ways to do it. You can write by hand on sheets of typing paper, or in a blank notebook or journal.

You can also type out your stories on a computer or a tablet. There are free word processing programs like Google Docs. You can save the work in cloud storage without needing your own computer.

You could also send yourself an email, typing your answers inside a message. Follow your interests and write one answer at a time if you wish.

If you want to tell stories out loud, you can audio record yourself or your loved ones. Send the audio file to a service like www.internettranscribers.com and they can convert it into text.

YOUR INFORMATION

Full Name at Birth:

_____

Date and Place of Birth:

_____

My Mother's Full Name and Maiden Name:

_____

My Mother's Date of Birth and Place of Birth:

_____

My Father's Full Name at Birth:

_____

My Father's Date of Birth and Place of Birth:

_____

What I know about My Grandparents:

_____

_____

FAMILY HISTORY: YOUR PARENTS

1. What are your parent's names and dates of birth?

2. How did your parents meet?

3. Did they talk about their dating years?

4. How did they become engaged?

5. If married, did your father ask permission to marry your mother?

6. Did he give an engagement ring?

7. Did they wear wedding bands?

8. Where did they get married?

9. Did they go on a honeymoon?

10. Are there any wedding photos?

11. What was the "something borrowed, something blue, something old" and "something new"?

12. Where did they live as newlyweds?

13. Did they have a car?

14. What stories did they tell you of their early years together?

15. What stories did they tell you about their own childhoods?

16. What cities did they grow up in?

17. Did they move?

18. Did they talk about their childhood games or activities?

19. Where did they go to school?

20. Did they finish high school?

21. Did they go to college?

22. Where did they go?

23. When did they graduate?

24. Do you know if they liked school?

25. What are your earliest memories of your parents?

26. How did they meet?

27. How long were they married/together when you were born?

28. What were the sayings or phrases they used most frequently?

29. Did they play games with you inside or outside?

30. Did they read to you or make up stories?

31. Did you ever see them argue?

32. Did you ever see them kiss?

33. How long did they live?

34. Where are they buried?

35. What was the highest level of education your parents received?

36. Did they want you to go to college?

37. Do you have any old family photos? Where are they?

38. What did you admire most about your parents?

39. Do you know anyone who knew your parents when they were young?

GRANDPARENTS

40. Where did your Grandparents grow up?

41. Did they always live in the United States?

42. Where else did they travel?

43. Why did your grandparents choose to marry?

44. How did they meet?

45. What stories did your grandparents tell you?

46. What did they tell you about their own childhood?

47. What did they tell you about their parents?

48. What did they tell you about their grandparents?

49. Did they tell you about any aunts or uncles?

50. Did they tell you any of their sibling's names, or where they were born?

51. What do you consider your grandparent's legacy to be?

52. Is that what they had hoped for their legacy?

IMMIGRATION

53. What were your grandparent's names, and dates of birth?

54. Where are your grandparents from?

55. Do you know how they came to the U.S.?

56. Did you hear any stories of the "old" country?

57. Were their names changed from the original spelling in their native language?

58. What did they bring with them on their journey?

59. How old were they when they immigrated?

60. What port did they arrive in?

61. Were they able to talk to their family back in their home country again?

62. Did they ever travel back for a visit?

63. What did they miss about their native country?

64. Did they speak another language?

65. Did they teach you any of their language?

66. Did they teach you to cook any dishes from their home country?

67. What do you think is most important about them coming from a "foreign" country?

68. What does it mean to you that they came from outside the U.S.?

OTHER RELATIVES

69. Have you ever researched your family roots?

70. Have you discovered distant cousins?

71. Do you have family that you didn't know about when you were younger?

72. If you were to reach out to those distant branches of the family tree, what would you want to know?

YOUR MEMORIES

73. What are some of your most distinct memories of your grandparents?

74. What did you learn from your grandparents?

75. Do you have any family heirlooms from them?

76. If you could ask your grandparents something today, what would you ask?

77. What holiday traditions do you carry on from your grandparents?

78. What jokes or sayings do you remember from your family?

ADOPTION

79. How old were you when you were you adopted?

80. Was anyone else in the family adopted?

81. What do you know about your birth family?

82. How old were you when you first knew your birth story?

83. How did you uncover the story?

84. How have you felt about being adopted, then and now?

85. At the time you were given up for adoption, you were a nameless baby without a personal identity. If it were possible to not feel personally rejected, what would than mean for your happiness?

YOUR PARENT'S PHILOSOPHY

86. What fun things did your parents do that your neighbors didn't do?

87. What surprises did your parents plan for you?

88. What made your family special?

89. How did your parents express their love to you?

90. What were your childhood nicknames?

91. Did your parents ever apologize to you for anything from your childhood?

92. How did your parents handle discipline?

93. Were there different rules for any of your siblings?

94. Did you think your parents were harder (or easier) on you than your siblings?

95. Were you in trouble often?

96. Did you earn an allowance?

97. What did your parents teach you about saving money?

98. What big purchase did you want to make with your saved allowance?

99. What did you get in trouble for as a kid that no one would care about today?

100. Did you ever get angry as a child?

101. What happened?

102. What parenting methods did you use as a parent yourself?

103. What beliefs were you raised with that have changed in families today?

104. What other relatives or friends of the family offered great advice when you became a parent?

CHILDHOOD GAMES AND ACTIVITIES

105. Did you ride a bicycle?

106. Who taught you how to ride?

107. Where did you go on your bike?

108. Did you ever receive a bicycle as a gift?

109. What did your bike look like?

110. Who gave it to you?

111. How long did you have it?

112. What happened to your favorite bike?

113. Did you ever take music lessons?

114. Did you learn to play an instrument?

115. Was practicing something you wanted to do, or were you forced to practice?

116. What games did you like to play?

117. What games did you play outside?

118. What games did you play in the summer?

119. In the winter, what games did you play inside?

120. Did you play any card games?

121. What was your favorite card game?

122. Did you play any board games?

123. What was your favorite?

124. What games did you like to play at school recess?

125. Did you ever have roller skates?

126. Did you ever have ice skates?

127. Did you ever play jacks?

128. Did you ever jump rope?

129. Did you ever play kick the can?

130. Did you ever play hide and seek?

131. Did you ever go camping as a child?

132. Where did you go?

133. Where did you sleep?

134. Do you get poison ivy?

135. Did you get sunburned?

136. What songs did you sing?

137. Did you have a campfire?

138. Did you see any shooting stars?

139. Did you ever catch fireflies (lightning bugs)?

140. Did you ever go away to camp?

141. Have you ever been lost in the woods?

142. Did you ever have a tree house?

143. Did you ever build a fort in the woods?

144. Did you ever go hunting?

145. Did you hunt with a bow and arrow or a gun?

146. What did you like about hunting?

147. Did you ever catch anything?

148. Did you clean the animal yourself?

149. Did you ever go fishing?

150. How old were you?

151. Did you clean the fish yourself?

152. Did you have family picnics?

153. Where did you go?

154. Was the picnic packed in a basket?

155. What did the carrying basket look like?

156. Did you use china plates or plastic?

157. What drinks were packed in the picnic?

158. What kind of cups did you use?

159. What kind of food was packed in the basket?

160. Did you sit on the grass, or a blanket?

161. Was there anything special about picnics?

162. Did you play any games while you were on a picnic?

163. What was the location of the picnic?

164. Tell me more about that location...

165. Have you returned to that spot as an adult?

166. Did your family take vacation trips?

167. What do you remember about a trip?

168. Did you have a bedtime routine?

169. Talk more about bedtime and what your remember

PETS

170. Did you have any pets growing up?

171. What kind of animals were they?

172. What were their names?

173. Did you ever save up and buy your own pet?

174. How old were you?

175. Did you ever dress up your pet?

176. Did your pet ever run away?

177. What was your favorite childhood pet?

178. Did you have to clean up after your pet?

179. Who fed and watered the pet?

180. Did you have to wash your pet?

181. Did you have to take your dog for walks?

GENERAL

182. Were you born in a hospital?

183. Which one?

184. Does that hospital building still stand?

185. What did your parents say about the day you were born?

186. What favorite objects did you carry in your pockets as a child?

187. Did you have any imaginary friends?

188. When did you learn to read? Who taught you?

189. What did you save up to buy with your money?

190. Did you receive money as birthday presents?

191. Where did you usually spend your allowance?

192. Did you have any secret hideouts?

193. Did you bury any treasure?

194. Did you learn any sports as a child?

195. How old were you when you learned to swim?

196. Were you in the boy scouts or girl scouts?

197. What do you remember doing as a scout?

198. Would you recommend that other children become scouts?

199. What secret did you promise a friend you would keep that now seems silly?

200. What trouble did you get into that you never were caught for?

201. What secrets did you keep for your siblings?

202. Did you ever run away?

203. Did anyone you know run away?

204. What was your favorite book to read?

205. Did anyone read to you?

206. Did anyone make up stories to tell you?

207. What was the first book that you owned?

208. Where did you get it?

209. Did you read to anyone else as a child?

210. Who taught you to print?

211. How old were you?

212. Did you have a textbook for printing?

213. Who helped you with tough times in school?

214. What in your childhood would you like to re-experience for just five minutes?

PERSONALITY

215. What about your childhood had the most impact on who you are today?

216. What did you like most about how you were raised?

217. What was your favorite thing to wear...was there an outfit you wanted to wear every day?

218. Did you suffer any serious illnesses as an infant or toddler?

219. Who do you think you are most similar to in your family? (Describe temperament and moods, etc.)

220. Do you feel these personality traits are positive or negative, and why?

221. How has your temperament helped you in your life?

222. Did you have any childhood nicknames?

223. How did you get that nickname?

YOUR FAMILY HOME

224. What were your chores?

225. Did you do any cooking?

226. How old were you when you learned to cook?

227. Did you have to wash or dry, or put away the dishes?

228. Did you earn an allowance?

229. What were the requirements to earn allowance?

230. How often were you paid allowance, and how much was it?

231. Were there any animals to care for?

232. Did your family have a television?

233. What were your favorite shows?

234. Where was your favorite place in the house?

235. Describe the room or place, and what you liked about it

236. Did you have ice, milk, bread, or eggs delivered to the house?

237. What was the delivery company's name?

238. How much did it cost?

239. What food was very special and rarely served?

240. What food did your parents always say NO to?

241. Was there one type of food (or one dish) that you wanted to eat exclusively?

242. What was your favorite dessert?

SAD TIMES

243. Were there any trips to the emergency room?

244. Who was the first person that died in your family?

245. How old were you at the time of their death?

246. Did you go to the funeral?

247. What do you remember about the funeral?

248. What do you regret about your childhood?

249. Did you ever rescue another child from injury or disaster?

250. Did your parents ever send you away? Why?

251. Did you ever call the police as a child? What happened?

252. Did your family ever need help from anyone?

253. Did a friend or family member ever disappear from your life?

254. Were any family members sentenced to jail time?

255. What happened?

256. Who meant a lot to you as a child, and then you lost touch with them?

SCHOOL

257. What time did you get up for school?

258. What did you usually eat for breakfast?

259. Did you have chores before leaving for school?

260. Did you cry on the first day of school?

261. Did your mother cry?

262. What else do you remember from the first day of school?

263. What did you wear to school?

264. Did they take class pictures?

265. Do you have any of your class pictures?

266. Who was your favorite teacher in grade school?

267. Did you take any field trips?

268. Did you ride the bus to school or did you walk?

269. Did your parents drop you off at school?

270. Did you like to study?

271. Were there any problem children in your class?

272. Who were your friends in primary school?

273. What games did you play together?

274. What did you talk about?

275. Have you kept in touch with any grade school friends?

276. Did you pack your lunch or was there a school cafeteria?

277. Who made your lunch?

278. Did you carry your lunch in a paper sack, a pail, or a metal lunch box?

279. Did you get milk at school?

280. Where did you eat your lunch?

281. What did your school look like?

282. How many students attended your school?

283. How many kids were in your class?

284. Was there a chalkboard in your classroom?

285. Were there inkwells built in to the desks?

286. Did anyone ever pass you a note in class?

287. Did you ever pass a note in class?

288. Were you caught?

289. Did you have to help clean the classroom daily or weekly?

290. Was there a recess or a lunch break?

291. Was there a playground?

292. What equipment was on the playground?

293. Was there a nap time or quiet time?

294. Is your primary school still standing?

295. Did you say the pledge of allegiance in the morning or start with prayer?

296. Did you ever get in trouble?

297. What was a memorable day at school?

298. What was your favorite day in school?

299. Did you have to memorize anything in school?

300. What was it?

301. Do you remember any of it now?

302. How often were there tests?

303. Was there a test that was memorable even today?

304. How has your childhood neighborhood changed?

TEEN YEARS AND FRIENDS

305. Who was your best friend?

306. What activities did you enjoy with your friends?

307. What activities did you prefer to do by yourself?

308. When did you notice romance?

309. How old were you when you were first allowed to date?

310. Who did you bring home for your parents to meet?

311. What happened at that first meeting?

312. Did your parents informally "adopt" any of your friends as their own?

313. Did you have groups of friends, or one or two close friends?

YOUR IDENTITY

314. What kind of school activities or groups were you involved in?

315. Were you a leader or a follower?

316. What were the standout moments of your teen years?

317. What would you do differently now if you'd "known better" then?

318. Did you suffer any serious illnesses as a teen?

319. Did you fight with your parents or siblings? About what?

320. Did you ever defend a anyone against a bully?

321. Did you ever come to someone's assistance in an accident or injury?

322. What was the situation?

323. What were you known for as a teen?

HIGH SCHOOL

324. Who was your favorite teacher?

325. Who was your best friend?

326. What did you do together after school?

327. What was your favorite year of high school?

328. What was your favorite class?

329. Did you learn to type in school?

330. Did you learn shorthand?

331. Did you have shop class, drafting, or metalwork?

332. Did you take biology or chemistry?

333. What games and activities were in physical education class?

334. Did you play any team sports?

335. Did you letter in any sports?

336. Did you play in orchestra or band?

337. Did you learn a foreign language?

338. Did you belong to any social clubs in high school?

339. What plans did you have for your future?

340. Did any of those high school dreams come true?

341. Did you get in trouble in high school?

342. What happened?

343. Were there any school trips that you went on?

344. What was a memorable day at school?

345. What was your favorite day of high school?

LOVE & DATING

346. When did you start dating?

347. How were you asked on your first date?

348. Who was your first date with and what did you do?

349. Were there any awkward first date moments?

350. Who was your first girlfriend/boyfriend?

351. How old were you?

352. Did your school offer homecoming or seasonal dances?

353. Were dances held in the school gymnasium or somewhere else?

354. What food or drinks were served?

355. Was there a live band?

356. What did you wear?

357. What song do you remember dancing to?

358. Who would you have missed meeting if things had been different by ten minutes?

359. Did you ever sneak out of the house?

360. Did you ever want to run away with someone?

361. What did your family think of your romantic interests?

362. What did your girlfriend/boyfriend think of your family?

YOUNG ADULTHOOD AND TRANSPORTATION

363. What was your first car?

364. Who taught you to drive?

365. What was your favorite car?

366. How did gasoline cost when you started driving?

367. What filling station did you use?

368. What services did they perform in addition to fueling?

369. Did you ever ride a motorcycle?

370. Own one?

371. Did you ever ride in a helicopter?

372. A hot air balloon?

373. Have you ever hitchhiked?

374. What car from the past do you wish you still had?

COLLEGE

375. Did you attend college?

376. Did you enjoy the experience?

377. How did you pay for school?

378. Did you have a job while in school?

379. What was your favorite class?

380. What was your field of study? Did it change?

381. Who did you meet there?

382. Who were your influential instructors, whom you still remember?

383. Where did you live while attending college?

384. Have you visited your college town since leaving?

385. Did you graduate?

386. What advice would you give to someone who's about to start school there?

387. Would you recommend they attend college at all?

388. What did you do socially on the weekends?

389. What activities from college do you wish you still participated in?

390. Did you take any road trips with friends?

391. Was there a favorite place at school where you liked to spend time?

392. What class do you wish you could take again today?

YOUR HOMETOWN

393. Where were you born?

394. Where did you grow up?

395. What has changed in the town since you were little?

396. Do you still have relatives there?

397. What happened to the house where you were born?

398. If you visited your childhood home as an adult, what did you think?

399. What was the local grocery store called?

400. Was there a special park or playground you would often visit?

401. Do you keep in touch with neighbors from your childhood?

402. Were there any newsworthy events or famous people from your hometown?

403. What do you miss about your hometown?

ENGAGEMENT

404. When did you first see your spouse?

405. How and where did you meet?

406. Who introduced you?

407. What was the date or time of year?

408. Where did you go on your first date?

409. When did you 'know' that this was going to be your spouse?

410. What was your parent's reaction to your engagement?

411. If you didn't tell them about your engagement, how did they react to your wedding?

412. How long were you engaged?

413. Were your parents supportive of your marriage?

414. What were the roadblocks you had to overcome before your wedding day?

415. What were your dreams about your wedding day?

416. Was there a bridal shower or bachelor party?

417. Who attended?

418. Did anyone try to break you up?

419. Did anyone warn you about marriage in general, or to your intended spouse?

420. How long did it take to plan your wedding?

421. What did you pay the church or Minister to perform your wedding?

422. Did you meet with him before the ceremony for counseling or to discuss marriage?

FOR BRIDES

423. What was your something old?

424. Your something new?

425. Something borrowed?

426. Something blue?

427. Did you wear a garter belt?

428. Did you wear a veil? What did it look like?

429. Describe your wedding dress and how you felt in it

430. How long did you keep your wedding dress?

431. Did anyone else wear your dress or veil for their wedding?

432. Were your shoes comfortable? Describe them

433. Who gave you away?

434. Did he have any words of advice just before you walked down the aisle?

435. What flowers were in your bridal bouquet?

436. If you tossed your bouquet, who caught it?

FOR GROOMS

437. Who proposed to whom?

438. How did you propose?

439. Did you offer an engagement ring?

440. Did you ask permission from her parents before proposing?

441. What questions did they have for you during that discussion?

442. Did you give her an engagement ring?

443. Where did you buy the wedding rings, and what did they cost?

444. Did you wear a wedding ring yourself?

445. What did you think or feel when you saw your bride coming down the aisle?

446. Who was the ring bearer?

447. Did anyone offer you any last minute advice?

WEDDING, RECEPTION AND HONEYMOON

448. Where did you get married? Was it in a church, private home, reception hall, outside, or somewhere else?

449. Who chose the wedding location?

450. Why did you choose that location?

451. What city or country was it in?

452. Who was your Best Man and Maid of Honor?

453. Did you follow the tradition of not seeing your betrothed before your wedding ceremony?

454. Where did you get ready for the wedding and who helped?

455. Did anything memorable happen during the wedding?

456. Was there live music or singing?

457. Did you save anything from your wedding?

458. Do you have any wedding photos?

459. Did you have a wedding reception?

460. Where was the reception and what did you serve?

461. Who offered toasts, and what did they say?

462. Did you have a wedding cake? Describe it

463. Did you make a grand entrance or exit from your reception?

464. Did you save a slice of wedding cake for later?

465. If you went on a honeymoon, describe it

IN-LAWS

466. Did your in-laws pass along any family secrets? Or
- recipes
- rumors
- warnings
- treasure maps
- stories about "bad blood" in the family

467. Who was the oldest member of their family?

468. What details do you remember of their family history stories?

469. Was there anyone you took on in their family as your own brother or sister?

470. What were some of your favorite things about your in-laws?

471. What went wrong with your in-laws or their extended families?

472. What's the funniest story you remember about them?

473. Did anyone give you any advice...good or bad?

474. Did anyone ever help out financially?

475. What were the circumstances?

476. Did you ever help anyone financially in your extended family?

477. How close to your house did your in-laws live?

478. Do you remember their street address?

479. What memory about them has stayed with you?

IDENTITY AND ORIENTATION

480. When did your same sex stirrings first emerge?

481. Who did you tell about your attractions?

482. How did others react when you told them?

483. What were you told growing up about same sex relationships?

484. Did you believe what you were taught when you were younger?

485. Did you ask your parents questions why they thought that way?

486. What was the discussion like when your shared your reality with them?

487. What did they say to you?

488. What did they ask you?

489. How did you feel after that first discussion?

490. Has anything changed over time?

491. Have you talked to your siblings about it?

492. Have you shared your identity with grandparents or cousins?

493. How were you influenced by others in your social circle?

494. Did you dress in a way that was accepted by your group, but rejected by society?

495. How has your style changed over the years?

496. How has your social group changed?

497. Who influences you the most?

498. How has society changed about their views and personal judgments?

499. What advice would you give a young person facing pressure to hide who they are?

ADULTHOOD

500. What age were you when you felt grown up?

501. Was there a specific moment you remember knowing you were an adult?

502. What changed in your outlook when you realized you could shape the direction of your life?

503. Were your political affiliations the same as your parents?

504. Who influenced your politics?

505. What was important to you as a young adult?

506. Who acted as a mentor for you?

507. Where did you meet your mentors?

508. What advice did you receive that is still useful today, and who gave you that advice?

509. What influenced your decision to move out on your own?

510. How old were you when you got your own place to live?

511. What address did you move to?

512. How did you feel when you moved out on your own?

513. Did you have roommates?

514. Did you invite your family to your new home for a meal or a visit? Describe

what happened on that first visit

515. How long did you live in your first place on your own?

PARENTING

516. How old were you when you became a parent?

517. Did you always want to have children?

518. How did you decide when to have children?

519. How did you decide what to name your children?

520. Were cigars given out at the birth?

521. Were your parents there for the birth of your children?

522. Were there any difficulties in pregnancy?

523. Did you enjoy pregnancy?

524. What did you do to get the house ready for a baby?

525. Was there a baby shower?

526. Were your children born in a hospital?

527. How did you choose the hospital?

528. What was the doctor's name who delivered your children?

529. How long did you stay in the hospital?

530. Were you given a general anesthetic?

531. How much was the hospital bill?

532. Did both parents sign the birth certificate?

533. Did anyone come and stay with you to help with the new baby?

534. What was your favorite stage or age in your children?

535. Did your babies sleep through the night?

536. Did you wash your own diapers?

537. Did you and your spouse both change diapers?

538. Did you sing to your babies?

539. What was the song?

540. What tricks did you use to soothe crying, or get them used to noise in the house?

541. Did you vacuum under the crib?

542. What worried you about becoming a parent?

543. Did you lose any children?

544. What have you always wanted to tell your children, but were hesitant to share?

545. Do you wish you had more children?

546. What's your favorite thing about being a parent?

547. What advice would you give to someone if they asked you about parenting?

OWNING A HOME AND DOMESTIC LIFE

548. Do you enjoy cooking?

549. What is your favorite thing to cook and to eat?

550. Where was the first house you bought?

551. How did you find the house?

552. How much was it and did you get any help from anyone for your down payment?

553. Describe any work you did on the house before moving in

554. Did you hire movers to help you?

555. What changes did you make to the house over the years?

556. What were your favorite changes?

557. What were the strange things that would happen around the house that you were always tinkering with?

558. How long did you live there?

559. Who were your neighbors?

560. Did you have a flower or vegetable garden?

561. Did you plant any flowers or trees?

562. Where else did you want to live?

LOSS

563. If you could get one thing back that was either lost or destroyed, what would it be?

564. What job did you want, but were never able to pursue?

565. What opportunity did you miss early in life that impacted who you are today?

566. Did it turn out to be a blessing?

567. What other doors were opened because of "missed" opportunities?

568. Did any of your friends or family members ever disappear?

569. Did you ever provide first aid to a stranger?

570. What "old fashioned" kitchen gadget do you wish you still had?

571. What would you say is the worst thing that ever happened to you in your life?

572. Who meant a lot to you, but you never told them?

573. Is there someone you wish that you had thanked back then?

574. Whose accomplishments are you proud of, but you never told them?

POLITICS

575. Who was your favorite politician in the U.S. or in the world?

576. Did you ever protest anything?

577. What was important to you about that cause?

578. Did you see any changes because of protesting?

579. Did you get into any legal trouble?

580. Do you remember segregation?

581. What did you think about the Korean War?

582. Do you remember where you were when President John F. Kennedy was shot?

583. Where were you when Reverend Martin Luther King was shot?

584. Where were you when we landed on the moon?

585. Where were you when President Ronald Reagan was shot?

586. Where were you on September 11, 2011?

587. Did you ever see or experience religious discrimination?

588. Against whom or what group?

589. What cause do you now donate time or money to?

HEALTH

590. How would you describe your overall health?

591. How much sleep do you need?

592. Are you an early riser or a night owl?

593. What time of day do you feel your best?

594. Do you enjoy regular exercise or other activities that energize you?

595. What are your secrets for feeling your best?

596. Did you ever have any serious illnesses or broken bones?

597. Have you ever donated blood?

598. Did you have any childhood illnesses or allergies that you grew out of?

599. What's your advice for a long and healthy life?

FEELINGS

600. Were you taught to express your feelings as a child?

601. When did this prove to be helpful?

602. How would you describe your usual mood as a child?

603. Were you ever jealous of any one?

604. Why?

605. What was a heartache you remember from your childhood?

606. Do you pay attention to your feelings now?

607. Did you ever attend counseling?

608. What did you think after your first session, was counseling helpful?

609. What did you learn about yourself in counseling?

610. What methods do you use to calm yourself and relieve stress?

611. Why are feelings important?

612. Do you ever follow gut feelings? What happens when you do? What happens when you don't?

FOOD AND EATING

613. What's your favorite food?

614. Did you ever try sushi?

615. Do you like seafood? What's your favorite kind?

616. Do you like desserts? What's your favorite?

617. Do you like to bake? What dish are you famous for cooking?

618. What food do you wish was on your plate right now?

619. Did you inherit any special family recipes?

620. Have you passed them on to anyone?

621. Who?

622. What dish from your parents or grandparents do you wish you could cook as well as they could?

623. What's your favorite meat dish?

624. How do you like steak cooked: rare, medium or well done?

625. What is the weirdest food you've ever eaten?

626. What food do you wish you'd never run out of?

627. What is your favorite snack?

628. Do you prefer salty or sweet things?

629. What family meal rituals do you have?

630. How often do you invite family or friends for dinner?

631. What do you like to cook for them?

632. If you could have a meal prepared for you right now, what would it be?

LOOKING BACK

633. What do you wish you could have asked your grandparents?

634. What sayings do you remember from your parents about money?

635. What sayings do you remember from your parents about love?

636. What sayings do you remember from your parents about work?

637. What sayings do you remember from your parents about family?

638. What do you wish you could know about your parents?

639. What was the best advice you were ever given?

640. What do you want your children to remember about you?

641. What should your children know about being aged in their sixties?

642. What should your children know about being in their seventies?

643. What should your children know about being in their eighties?

644. What should your children know about being in their nineties?

645. What should your grandchildren know about their parents?

646. What advice do you have for your grandchildren about making decisions for themselves?

647. If you could talk with a historical figure for thirty minutes, who would it be?

648. What famous people have you met?

649. What were the circumstances?

650. Did you talk with them?

651. What was said?

652. Did you get a photo or autograph at the time?

653. What did you think about them after you met them? Did your opinion of them change?

654. What decisions have you made that you would change if you could?

655. What's the happiest moment in your life?

656. How has your outlook and attitude affected your life?

PERSONALITY

657. How would you describe yourself to someone who doesn't know you?

658. What is your general mood and disposition most of the time?

659. Describe a time you were really happy

660. When have you been really angry? Describe the situation.

661. Now as a mature adult, what have you learned about feelings and how they work?

662. Who do you know who is exactly like you?

663. Do you think that personalities change over time?

664. Who do you wish you could be more like? Who do you admire?

665. Do you ever get nervous around people and hide the real you?

WEATHER

666. What's your favorite kind of weather and why do you enjoy it?

667. How do you feel when you are experiencing your favorite type of weather?

668. What do you least enjoy?

669. What don't you like about it?

670. What outdoor temperature is your favorite?

671. What do you like to wear in that temperature?

672. When did you first experience air conditioning?

673. What is your favorite kind of heating? (wood fires, gas heat, electric heat, LP gas, etc.)

674. Did you ever experience a solar eclipse?

675. When was it and what was it like?

676. Do you ever get angry at the weather?

677. What's your favorite thing about each season of the year and why?

678. If you could have one season last all year round, what would it be?

RECREATION AND GOING OUT

679. Did you enjoy going out to eat?

680. What is your favorite restaurant?
   - Your favorite dish they serve?
   - Do you know the staff or the owner very well?
   - Do you prefer to pick up food and eat at home?
   - Do you ever order dessert?
   - Which restaurant has the best dessert?

681. How often do you go out to eat?

682. Do you like to play card games?

683. Who taught you how to play cards?

684. What's your favorite deck of cards or manufacturer?

685. Do you play board games?

686. What's your favorite?

687. Do you like crossword puzzles, word search, math games or other puzzles?

688. Did you ever play horseshoes?

689. Where were you when you played outdoor games?

690. Did you every play croquet?

691. Did you ever play badminton?

692. Did you every play frisbee?

693. Did you like to go to the movies?

694. What is your favorite movie of all time?

695. What movie have you seen more than once?

696. Who is your favorite movie star and why?

697. Do you like to read magazines about movie stars?

VACATIONS

698. List your most memorable trips, and when you visited

699. What was your favorite trip? Describe why it was wonderful

700. Who traveled with you and who did you meet there?

701. Do have any pictures from vacation?

702. What happened on a trip that you still remember today?

703. What did you purchase while traveling that you still have now?

704. Where did you hope to visit, but never went?

705. Why did you want to go there?

706. How often did you go on vacation?

707. Did you enjoy traveling, and why?

708. Did you send any telegrams or postcards when traveling?

NATURE

709. Did you ever raise a garden?

710. What grew the best for you?

711. What was your favorite thing to plant?

712. Did you ever preserve or can your produce?

713. Did you bake any fruit pies?

714. How did you till the garden?

715. Did you mix in manure?

716. Where did the fertilizer come from?

717. Did you ever have livestock?

718. What kind?

719. Did you name your animals?

720. Did you ever ride horses?

721. What animals have you seen in the wild?

722. Have you ever been hiking or backpacking?

723. Where in the world do you want to be during your favorite season?

724. What makes it special for you?

725. What National Parks have you visited?

726. What was your favorite park?

727. Describe what made the trip so memorable

728. What is the most amazing thing you have seen outside?

MUSIC AND THEATER

729. What is your favorite musical band or performer?

730. Have you ever see them perform live?

731. Do you enjoy plays or musicals?

732. What were some memorable moments of theater for you?

733. Have you ever visited backstage?

734. Do you still have any playbills or programs?

735. What theater was your favorite to attend?

736. Did they serve refreshments?

737. How did you get there? By bus or car?

738. Is the theater still standing?

739. What did you enjoy most about live performances?

740. Did you ever play in a band or do something from the stage?

MILITARY: SERVING OUR COUNTRY

741. How long were you in the military?

742. Were you drafted or did you enlist?

743. How did you feel about it?

744. How did your family react?

745. Were you frightened?

746. Did you keep in touch with any service buddies?

747. What did you miss most about the comforts of home?

748. Did you receive any care packages?

749. Did you have a favorite ration?

750. What were your duties?

751. What else should we know?

752. What happened to your dog tags?

753. Did you keep any souvenirs from military travel?

754. Who did you meet in your service tours?

755. What was the most beautiful thing you saw while serving?

756. Have you attended any reunions?

757. Have you been honored for your service after leaving active duty?

758. Does anyone ever ask about your service?

759. Do you like to talk about it?

760. What's your favorite story about service?

761. What should we know about wartime?

762. What should we know about occupying foreign countries?

763. What needs to change in the military?

764. What needs to remain tradition in the military?

GADGETS AND TELEVISION

765. What gadgets do you have now that you didn't have growing up?

766. Who was the first person you knew with a television set?

767. How much did it cost?

768. What programs did you watch on TV?

769. What's your favorite show from the past?

770. When you think of TV now, what specifically has changed in television?

771. What's your favorite TV show now?

772. What do you wish you could see on TV again?

FIRST JOB

773. What was your first job?

774. How did you hear that they needed help?

775. Were you interviewed?

776. What questions did they ask?

777. What was your starting pay?

778. How frequently were you paid?

779. What did you spend your first paycheck on?

780. Did you receive any pay raises?

781. How long did you work there?

782. What did you learn about yourself?

783. What lessons did you learn about work in general?

784. Is that company still in business?

WORK

785. Did you ever work in an office?

786. Did you ever start a company?

787. What did you like about your employment?

788. What jobs have you had?

789. What were your wages?

790. Do you have any paystubs from previous employers?

791. Why did you keep them?

792. Were there any office politics?

793. Who were your favorite people at work?

794. What changes do you wish you could've made at work?

795. What was your favorite job, and why?

796. What was your most difficult day at work?

797. Assuming you're retired now, what did you love about working?

TRAVELING FOR WORK

798. Did you ever go on a business trip?

799. Where did you go?

800. When was the trip?

801. How did you get there?

802. How long were you there?

803. What do you remember about the city?

804. What do you remember about the people?

805. Did you call anyone at home while you were on the trip?

806. Where did you dine when you were traveling?

PROFESSIONAL HISTORY

807. What was the first job you had outside of household chores?

808. How long did you work there?

809. Did you learn anything?

810. Did you make any friends there?

811. What job did you have that no one else wanted?

812. What is the strangest job you ever had?

813. Where did you work the longest?

814. What kept you working there for that long?

815. What were your duties?

816. Who did you report to?

817. Who were your co-workers?

818. How long did it take to get to work?

819. Did your family support you in your work there?

820. Did you stay in touch with anyone from that time?

821. Why did you leave?

822. Did you receive any recognition when you left? (A party, a gift, etc.)

823. What job did you hold for the shortest time?

LIFE PURPOSE

824. What are you grateful for?

825. Do you feel that you've followed your life's mission so far?

826. What needs to change inside of you (if anything) to live a life that you love?

827. If anything was possible, what part of your life would you let go of in order to be happier ?

828. What are you fearful of? Why is it hard to let go of that fear?

829. What seems to get in your way of living the life that you want?

830. What do you still absolutely need to have, need to do, or accomplish?

831. If you had the power or knowledge to solve a pressing problem in the world, and unlimited resources, what issue would you resolve first?

832. Why is this issue important to you?

833. What advice is important for young people to know?

834. What do you feel you still need to work on in yourself?

FAITH

835. What does "faith" mean to you?

836. Why is having faith important or not important to you?

837. How do you feel about organized religion?

838. How would you describe your belief about God?

839. What should people have faith in?

CHURCH

840. Did your parents take you to church when you were little?

841. What was church like?

842. Did you sing along with the congregation or ever sing in the choir?

843. Did you play an instrument in church?

844. What did you usually wear to church?

845. What do you remember about the pastor?

846. Were you baptized as an infant or young child?

847. Were there social gatherings at church?

848. Did you attend church as a family?

849. Where did you attend?

850. When and where were you baptized?

851. Did you ever go on any mission trips in the U.S. or abroad?

852. Did you ever participate in bible study?

853. Were you ever in a prayer group or social groups?

854. Who has been your favorite pastor, and what is special about them?

855. What's your favorite thing about church?

GOD

856. Why do you think God created you at this point in human history?

857. What is your earliest memory of God?

858. Have you ever seen God or heard God's voice?

859. Have you ever seen Angels?

860. How do you like to pray?

861. Are there prayers you say every day (like the Lord's Prayer, etc.)

862. Do you review the events of your day before bedtime?

863. What has God said to you directly, or through other people?

864. Where do you think that God really lives?

865. What do you tell God?

866. What does God think about you?

867. What do you wish others knew about God?

AFTERWORD

If you can ask just one question today, you'll make a difference. Be present for someone by looking into their eyes and listening. It's the greatest gift you can give.

OTHER WAYS TO USE THESE QUESTIONS

- Use as conversation starters to deepen your relationship with elder family members
- Create fictional character traits and details for novels or screenplays
- Choose three questions and answer them from the perspective of someone you may be having trouble communicating with right now
- Ask your partner some of these questions
- Use these with people who are in senior living or memory care centers to record the story of their life

ABOUT THE AUTHOR

Christina Dreve Young coaches aspiring authors of fiction, non-fiction, memoir, and entrepreneurs who want to attract more clients with a book. Christina provides a step-by-step process, support, and encouragement from idea phase to publishing.

Want to receive a new writing prompt every week? Join the *Tuesday Writing Club* at www.GetYourBookStarted.com.

Christina lives in a five-acre wood east of Cincinnati, Ohio with her husband Glen, and their pets Chica and Pickles.

Other Books by Christina Dreve Young available on Amazon.com:

Adventure Journaling: A Compass for Self-Discovery

My Feelings Journal: With Guided Exercises and a
Word Bank of 2000 Emotions

Rides to Remember: A Motorcycle Log Book

Write Your First Book in 30 Days: Get Ready, Get Support, and Get Writing

Write Your Novel in November: Last-Minute Mind Tricks and
Shortcuts I've Learned from NaNoWriMo

www.ingramcontent.com/pod-product-compliance
Lightning Source LLC
Chambersburg PA
CBHW080558030426
42336CB00019B/3243